Easy Piano CD Play-Along

INCLUDES CD

Orchestrated arrangements with you a[s]

LOVE SONG FAVORITES

T0041183

ISBN 0-634-05085-0

HAL•LEONARD® CORPORATION

7777 W. BLUEMOUND RD. P.O. BOX 13819 MILWAUKEE, WI 53213

Visit Hal Leonard Online at
www.halleonard.com

CONTENTS

FIELDS OF GOLD

Written and Composed by
G.M. SUMNER

Flowing, moderately

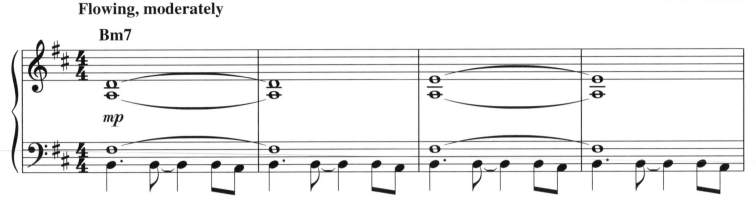

You'll re-

mem-ber me ___ when the west wind moves ___ up-on the fields ___ of
stay with me, ___ will you be my love ___ a - mong the fields ___ of

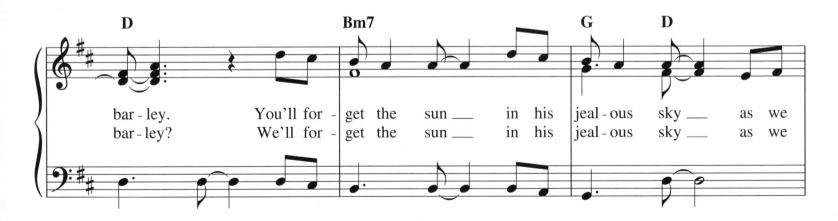

bar - ley. You'll for - get the sun ___ in his jeal-ous sky ___ as we
bar - ley? We'll for - get the sun ___ in his jeal-ous sky ___ as we

5

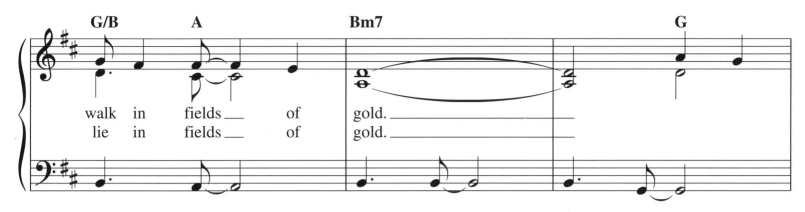

walk in fields ___ of gold. _____
lie in fields ___ of gold. _____

So she took her love ___ for to
See the west wind move ___ like a

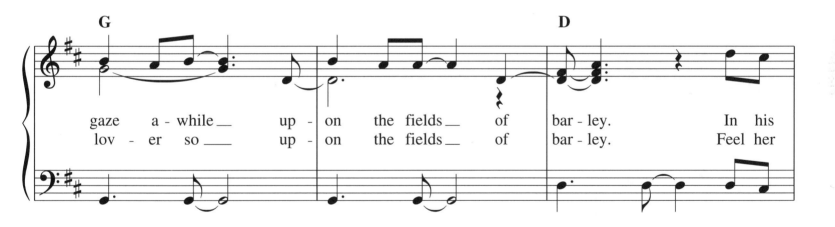

gaze a - while ___ up - on the fields ___ of bar - ley. In his
lov - er so ___ up - on the fields ___ of bar - ley. Feel her

arms she fell ___ as her hair came down ___ a - mong the fields ___ of
bod - y rise ___ when you kiss her mouth ___ a - mong the fields ___ of

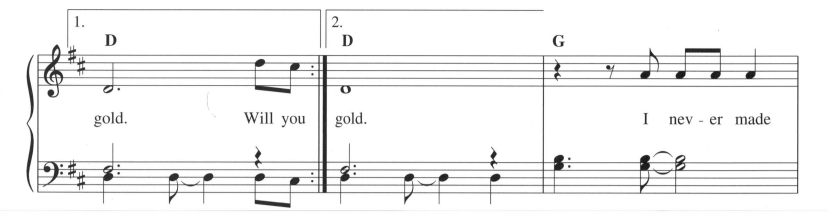

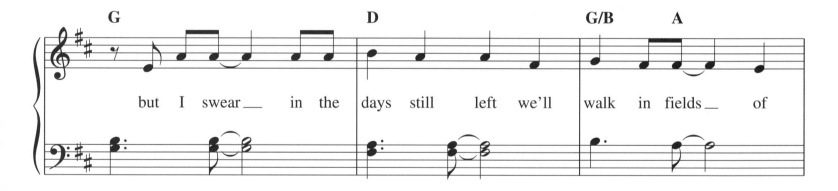

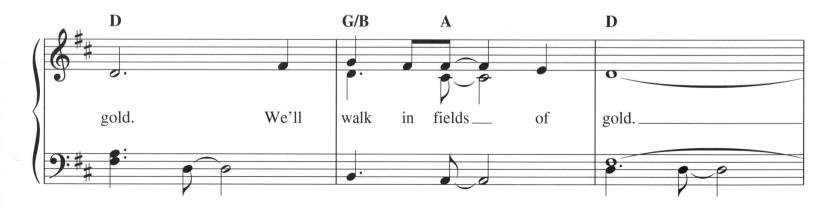

7

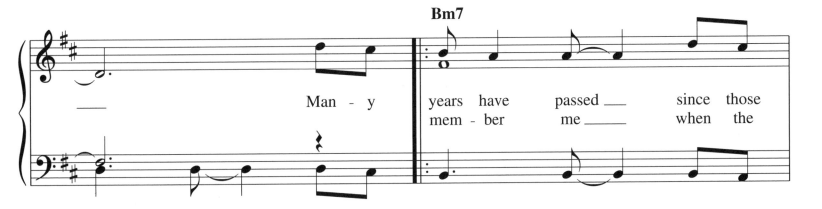

Bm7

Man - y years have passed ___ since those
mem - ber me ___ when the

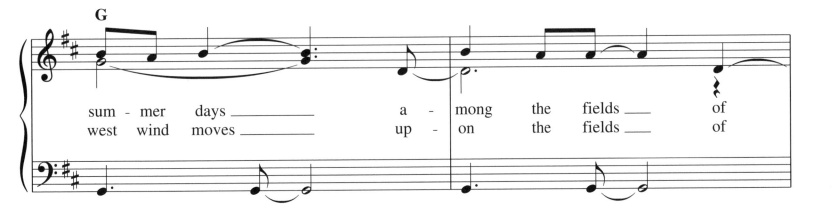

G

sum - mer days ___ a - mong the fields ___ of
west wind moves ___ up - on the fields ___ of

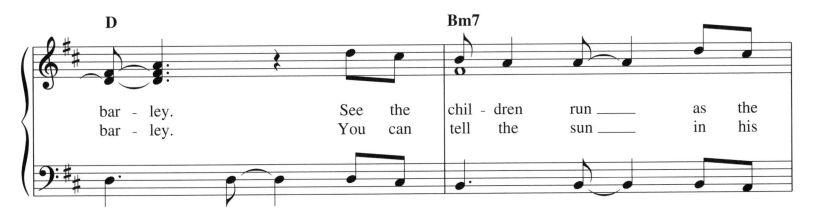

D   **Bm7**

bar - ley. See the chil - dren run ___ as the
bar - ley. You can tell the sun ___ in his

G   **D**   **G/B**   **A**

sun goes down ___ a - mong the fields ___ of
jeal - ous sky ___ when we walked in fields ___ of

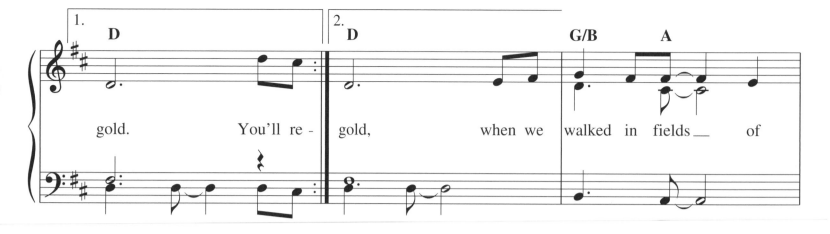

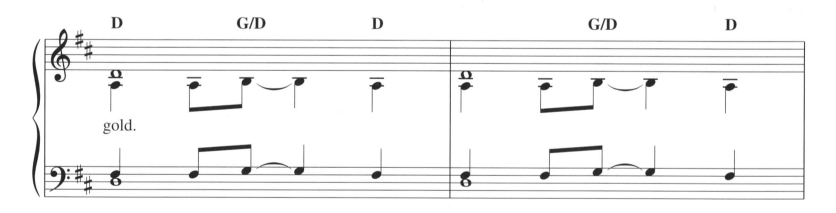

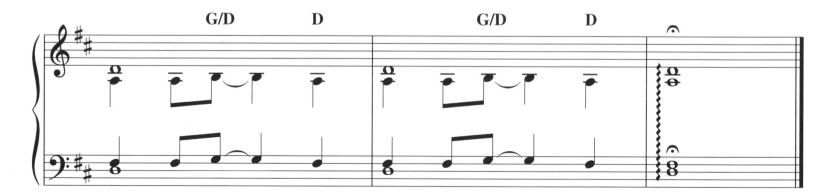

IF

Words and Music by
DAVID GATES

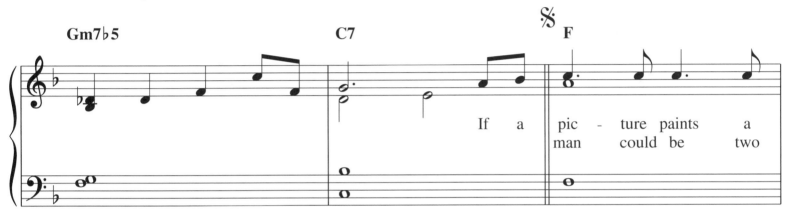

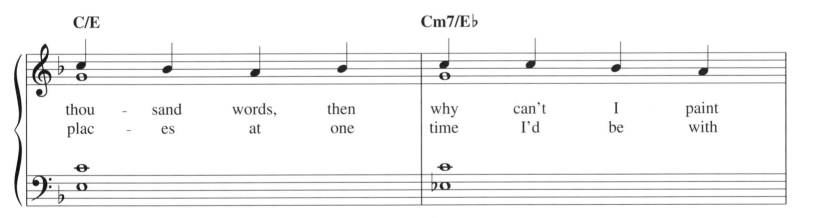

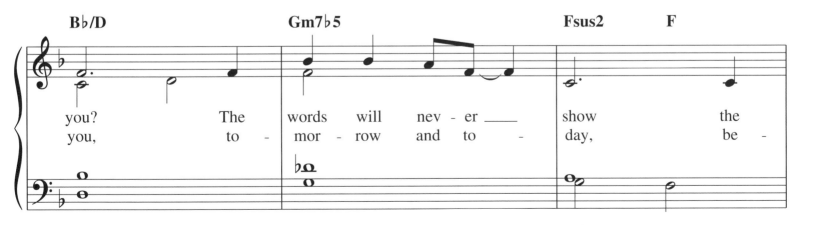

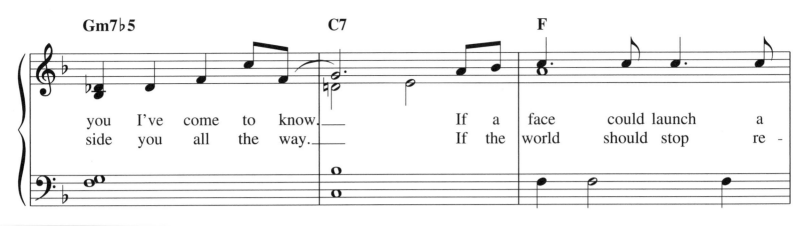

you I've come to know.___ If a face could launch a
side you all the way.___ If the world should stop re-

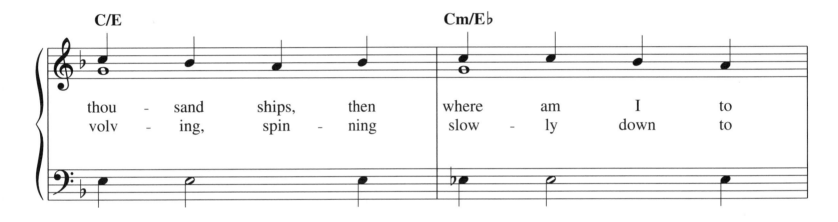

thou - sand ships, then where am I to
volv - ing, spin - ning slow - ly down to

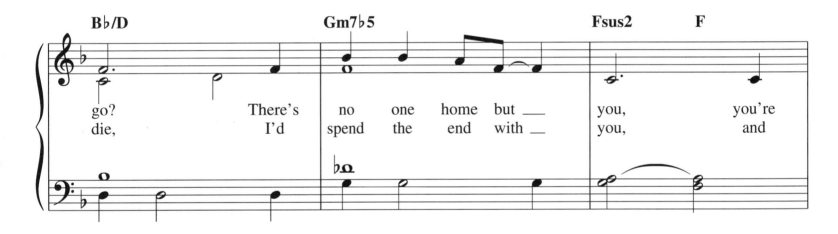

go? There's no one home but ___ you, you're
die, I'd spend the end with ___ you, and

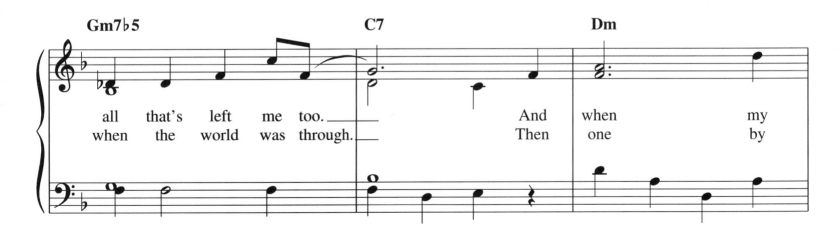

all that's left me too.___ And when my
when the world was through.___ Then one by

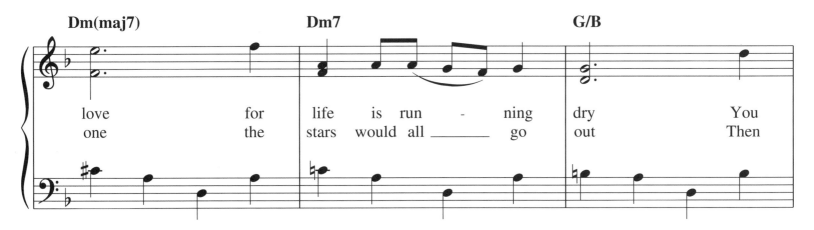

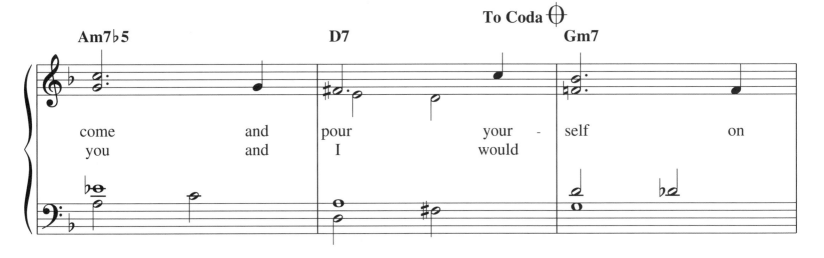

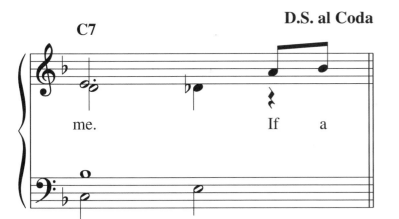
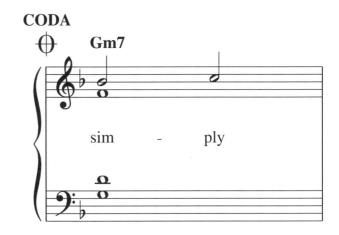

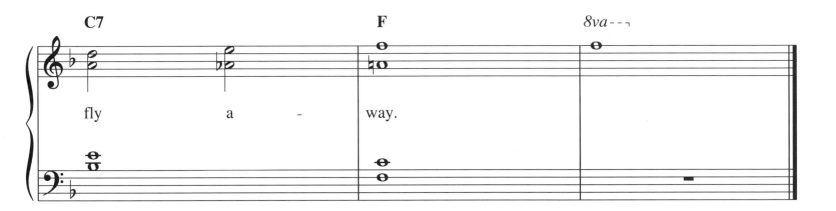

I HONESTLY LOVE YOU

Words and Music by PETER ALLEN
and JEFF BARRY

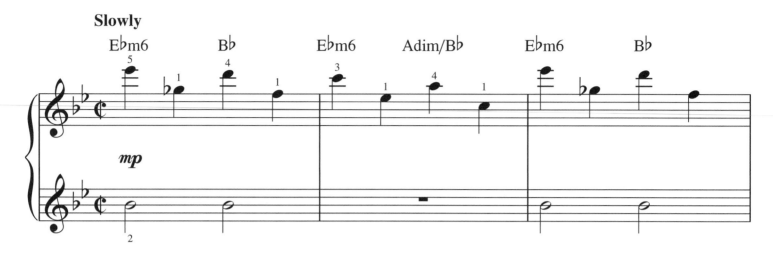

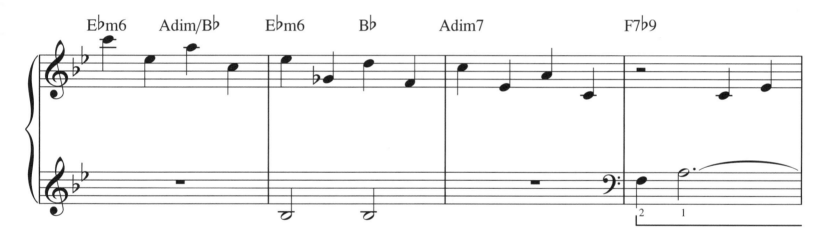

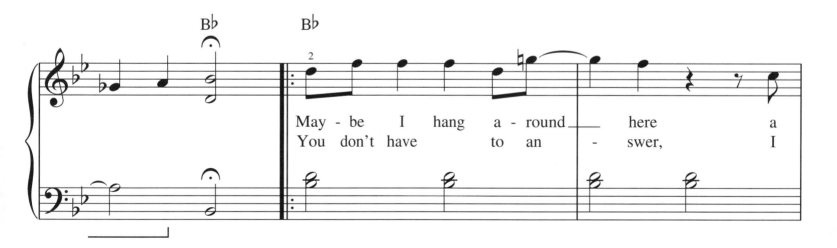

May - be I hang a - round___ here a

You don't have to an - swer, I

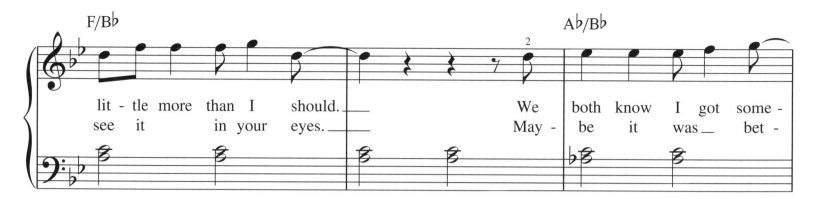

lit - tle more than I should. ___

see it in your eyes. ___

We both know I got some -

May - be it was ___ bet -

- where else ___ to go.

- ter left ___ un - said.

But

But

I got some - thin' to tell ___ you that I nev - er thought ___ I would,

this is pure ___ and sim - ple and you must re - a - lize

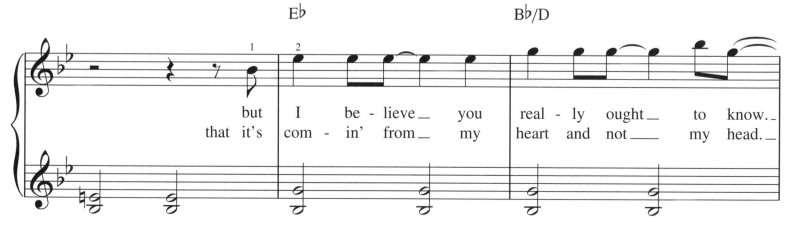

but I be - lieve ___ you real - ly ought ___ to know. ___

that it's com - in' from ___ my heart and not ___ my head. ___

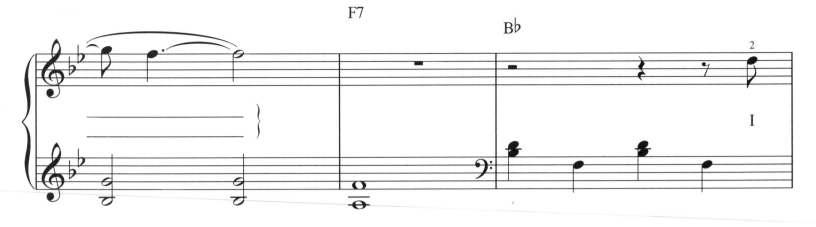

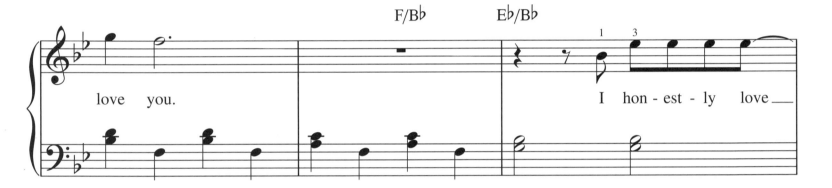

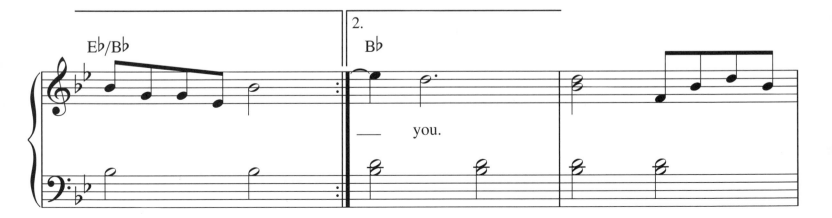

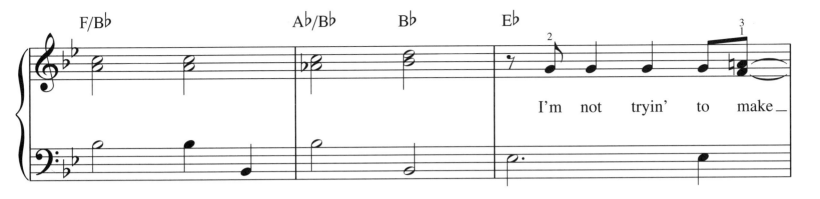

I'm not tryin' to make___

___ you feel___ un - com - f'ta - ble.___ I'm

not tryin' to make you an - y - thing___ at all,

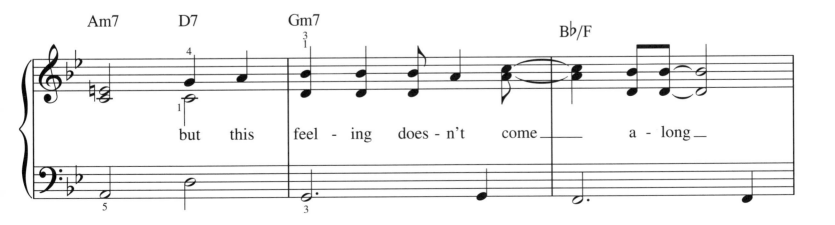

but this feel - ing does - n't come_____ a - long___

F/E♭   E♭

ev - 'ry day, _____ and you should - n't blow __ the chance __

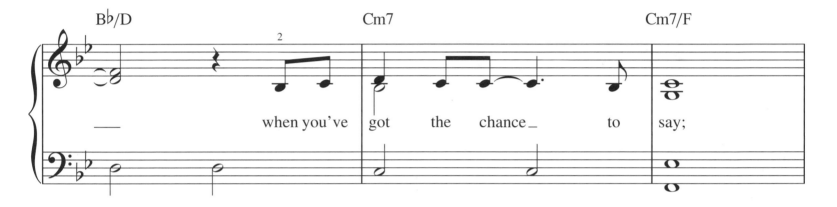

B♭/D   Cm7   Cm7/F

_____ when you've got the chance __ to say;

B♭   F/B♭

I love you.

E♭/B♭

Spoken: I love you.

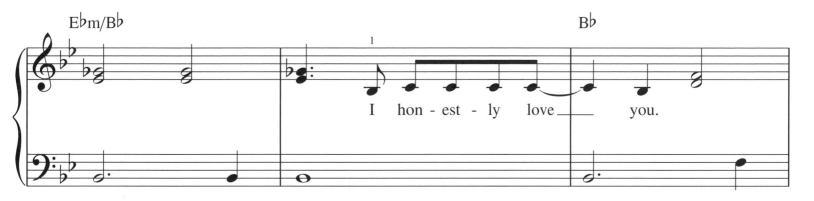

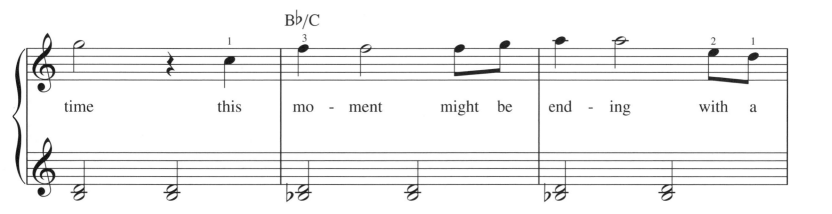

kiss,   but there you are   with

yours   and here I am   with mine,   so I

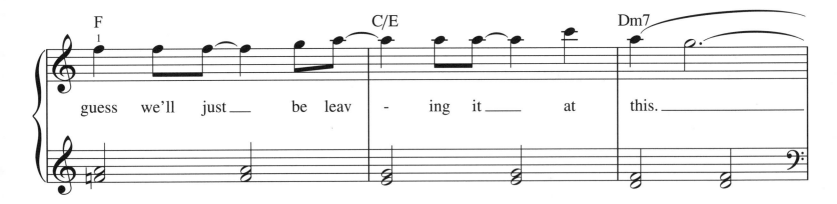

guess we'll just   be leav - ing it   at   this.

                                              I love you.

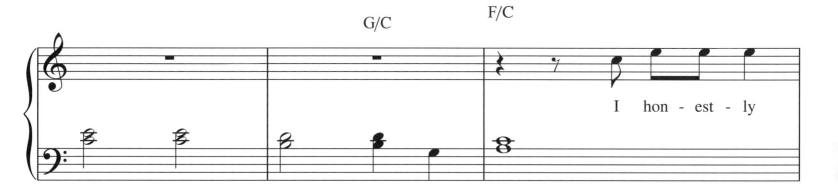

LADY IN RED

Words and Music by
CHRIS DeBURGH

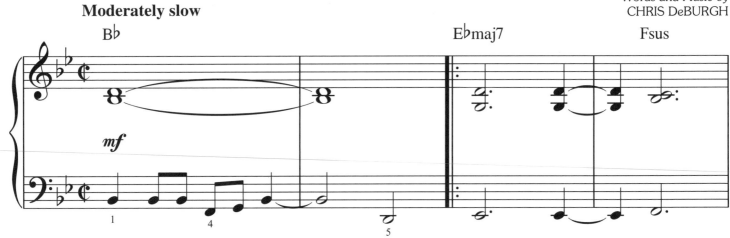

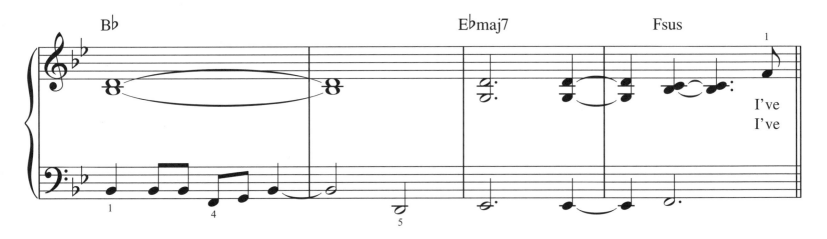

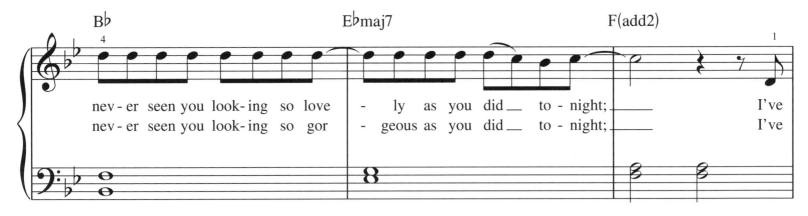

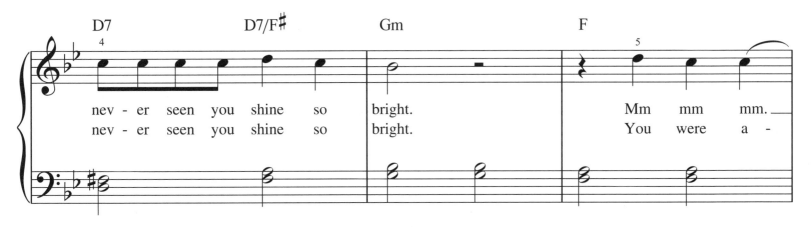

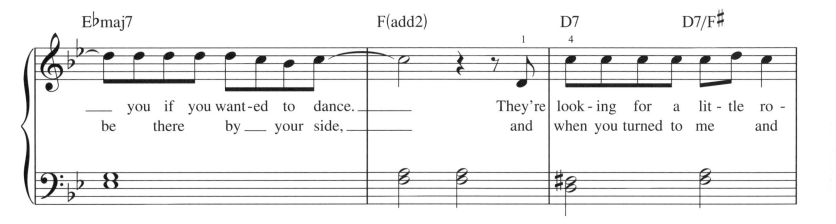

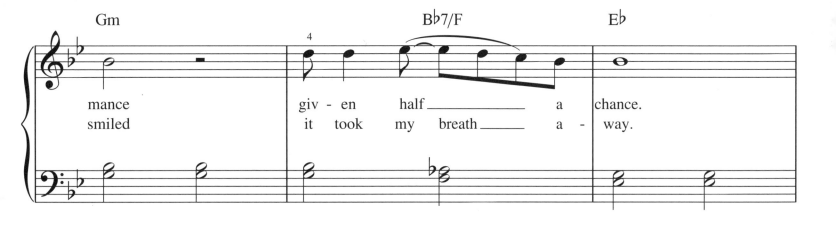

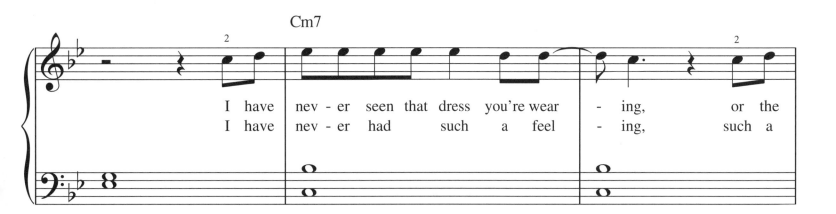

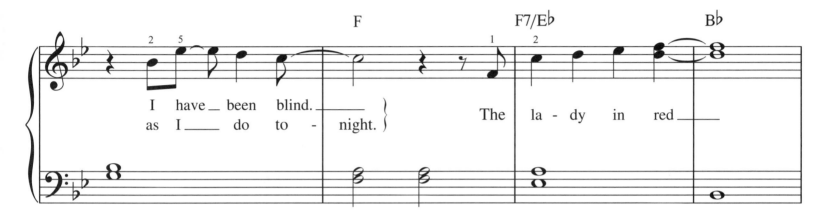

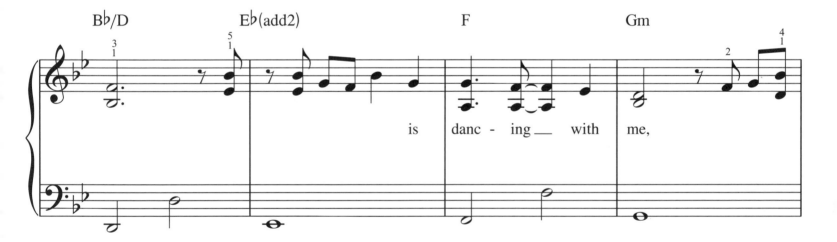

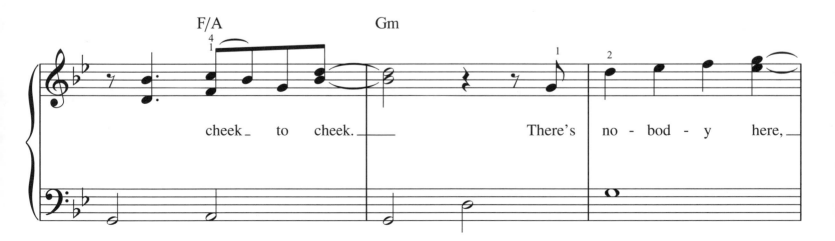

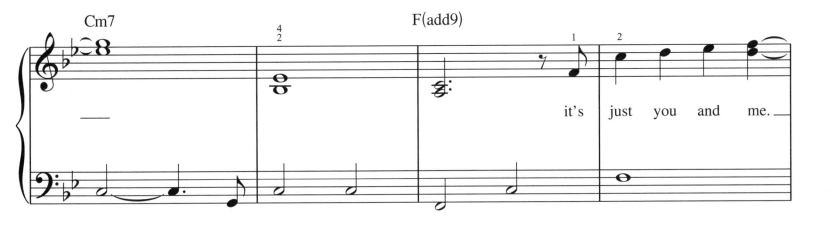

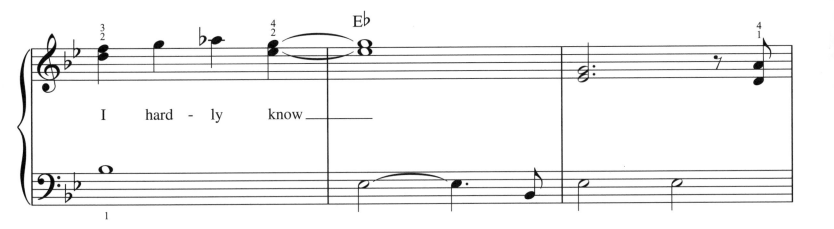

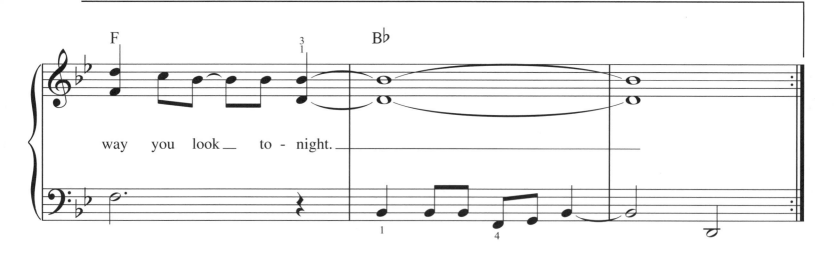

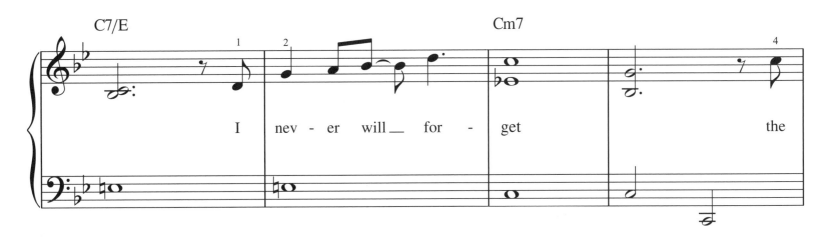

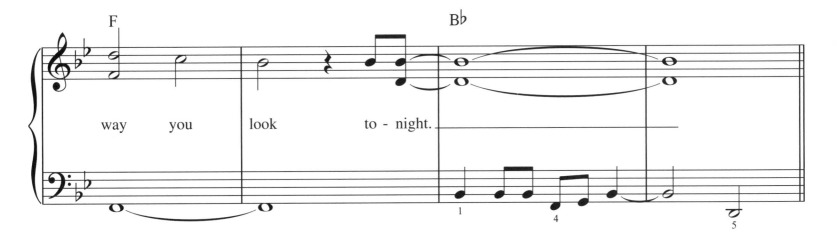

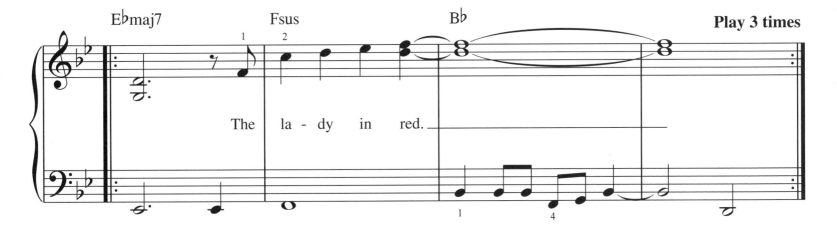

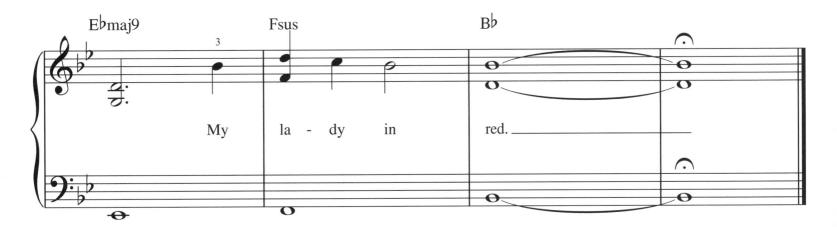

MORE THAN WORDS

Words and Music by NUNO BETTENCOURT
and GARY CHERONE

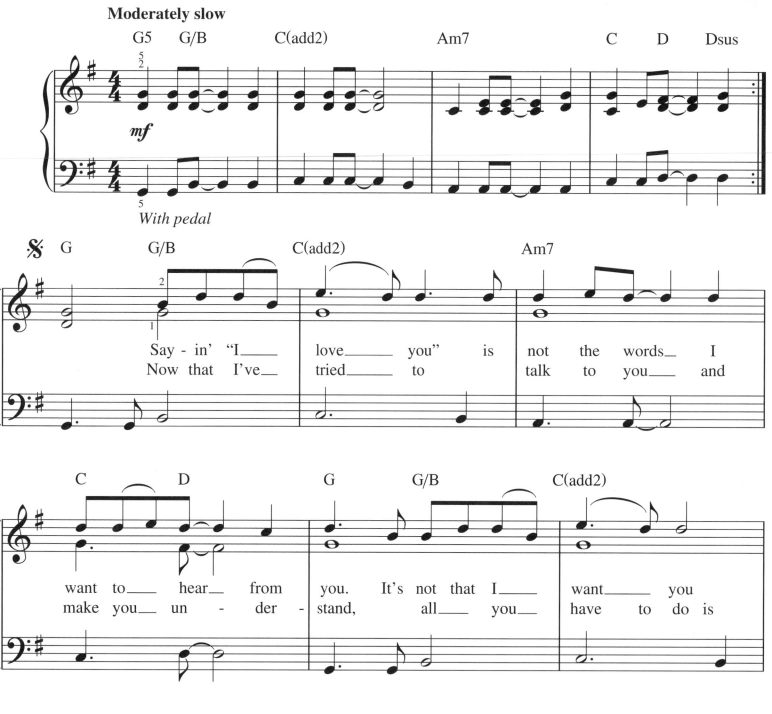

Say - in' "I____ love____ you" is not the words____ I
Now that I've____ tried____ to talk to you____ and

want to____ hear____ from you. It's not that I____ want____ you
make you____ un - der - stand, all____ you____ have to do is

not to say,____ but if you____ on - ly____ knew how____ and____
close your eyes____ and just reach____ out____ your____ hands____ and____

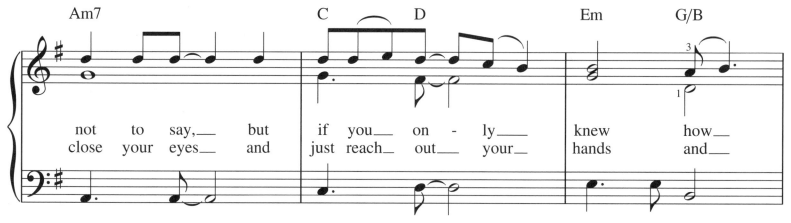

eas - y_____ it would be___ to___ show me how__ you

touch me.____ Hold me close, don't ev - er let___ me

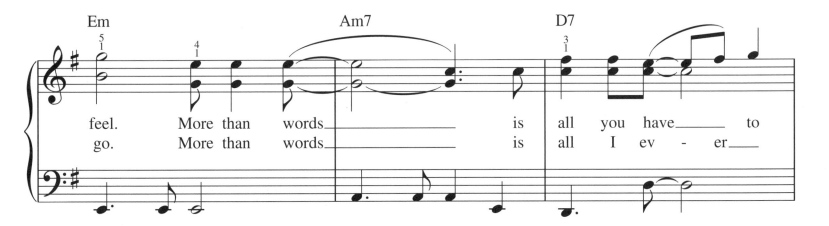

feel. More than words_____ is all you have_____ to

go. More than words_____ is all I ev - er____

do to make__ it____ real. } Then you would - n't have to say___

need - ed you__ to____ show.

_____ that you love___ me_____ 'cause I'd_____ al -

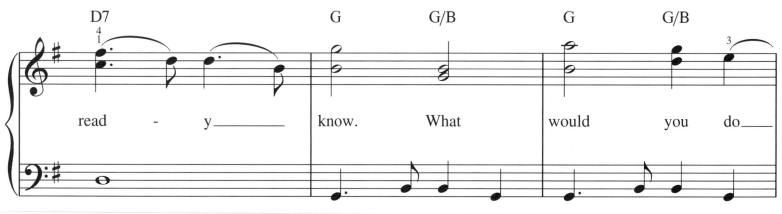

read - y_____ know. What would you do_____

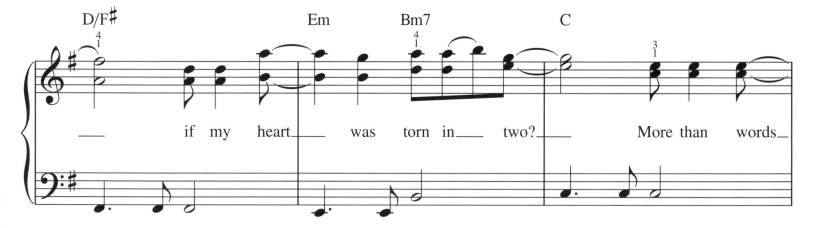

_____ if my heart____ was torn in____ two?____ More than words____

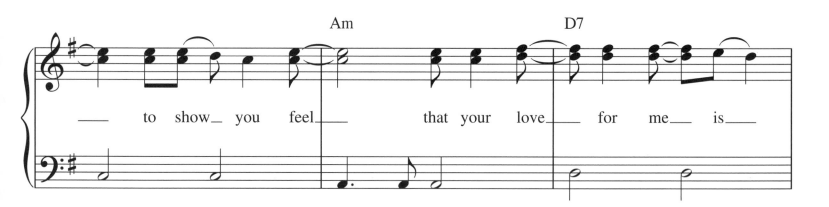

_____ to show_ you feel____ that your love____ for me___ is____

real. What would you say____ if I took____

those words a - way? Then you could - n't make things new

To Coda ⊕

just by say - in' "I love you."

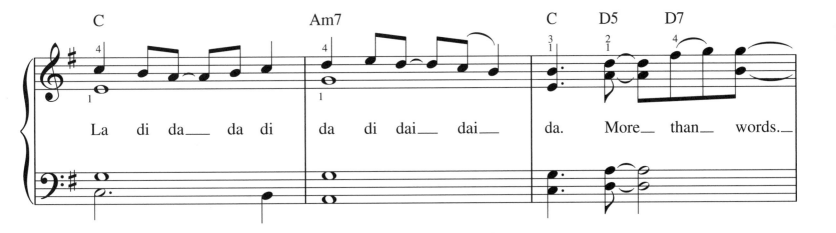

La di da da di da di dai dai da. More than words.

D.S. al Coda

La di da da di da.

CODA

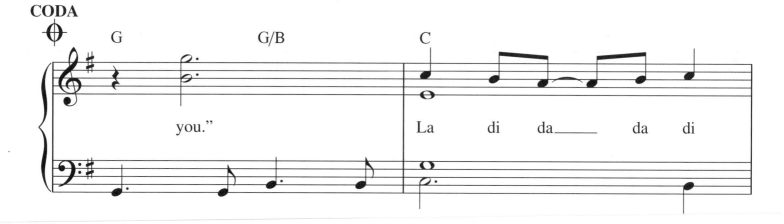

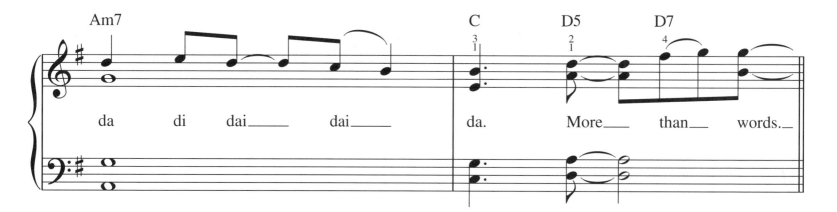

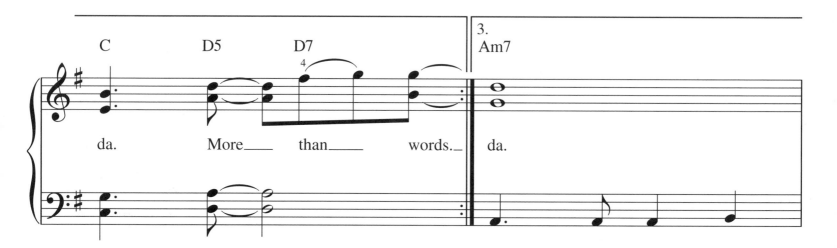

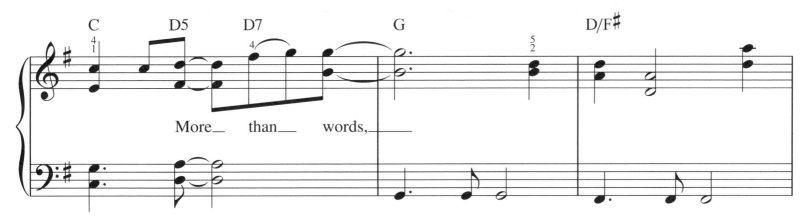

More_ than_ words,_

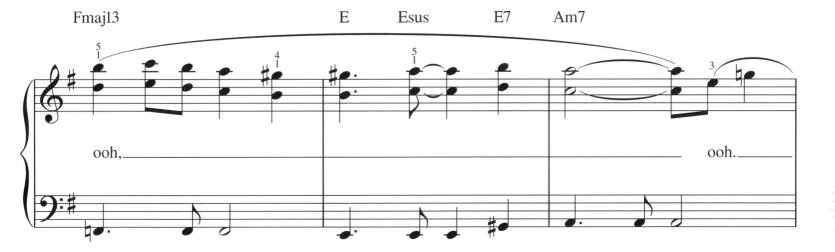

ooh,_____ ooh._

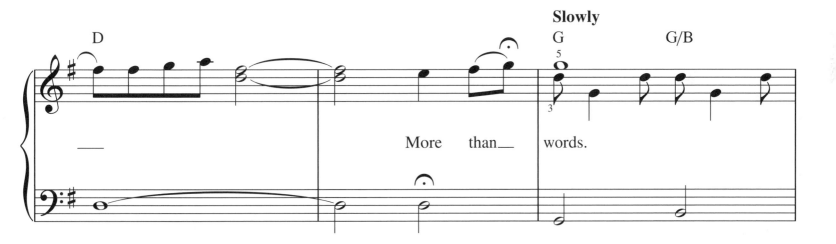

More than_ words.

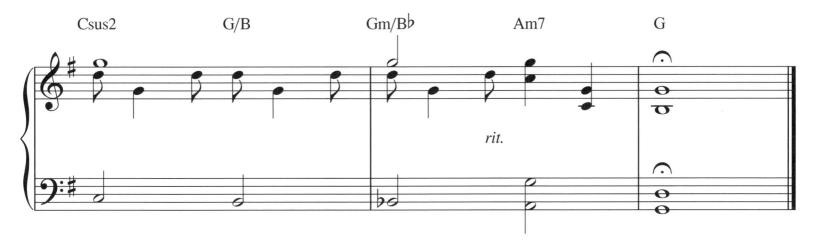

rit.

SAVE THE BEST FOR LAST

Words and Music by PHIL GALDSTON,
JON LIND and WENDY WALDMAN

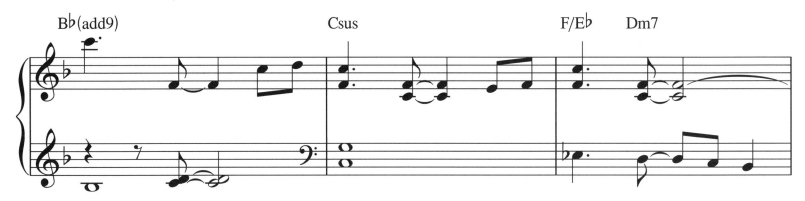

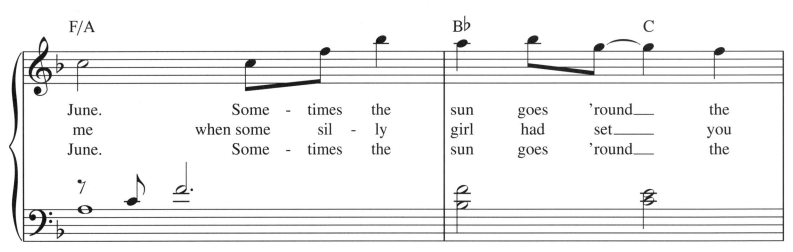

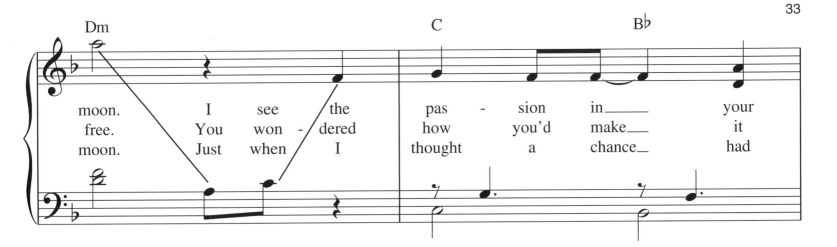

To Coda ⊕

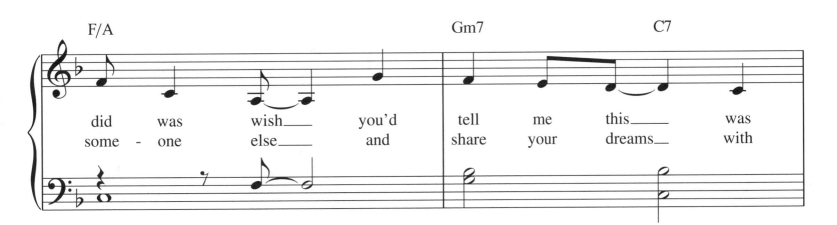

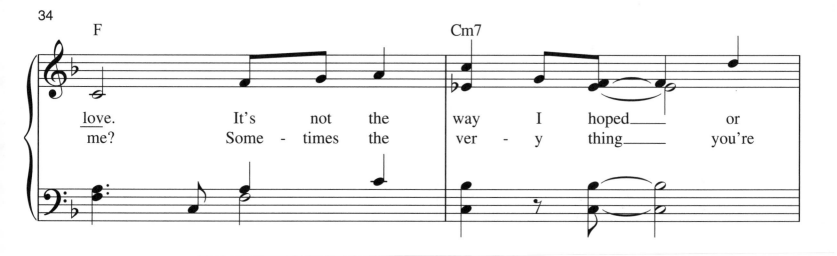

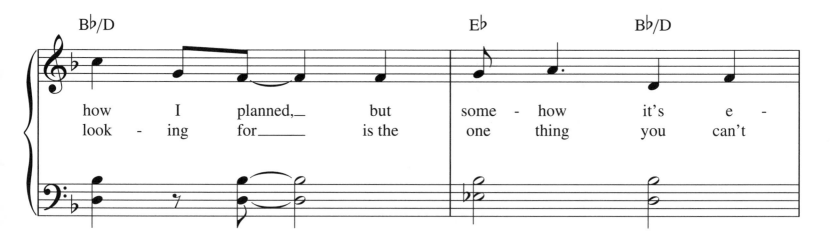

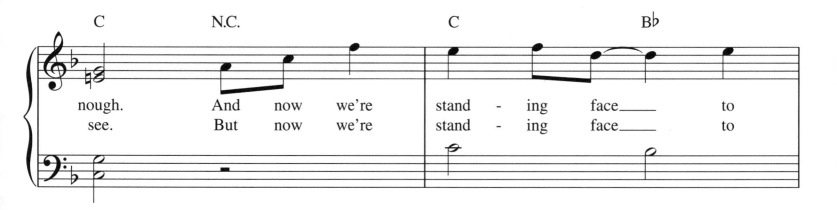

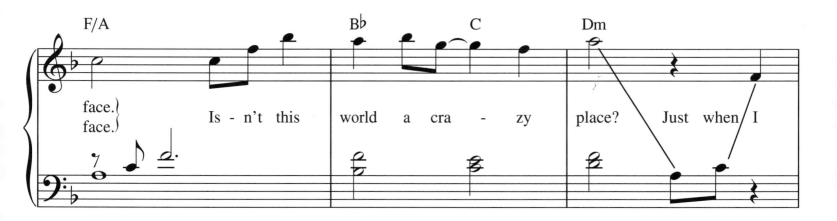

35

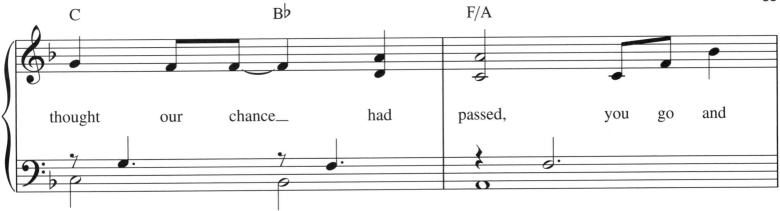

thought   our   chance___   had   passed,   you   go   and

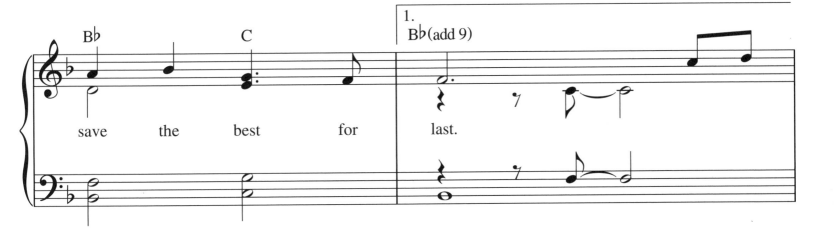

save   the   best   for   last.

All   of   the   last.

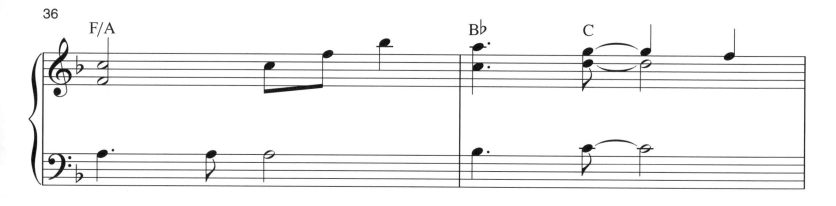

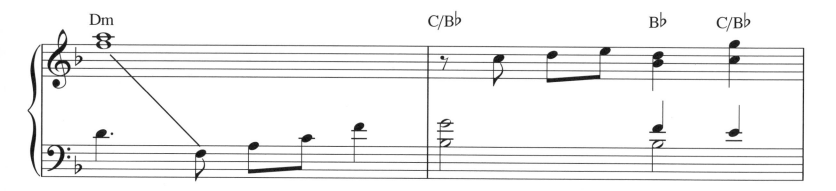

Some - times the

ver - y thing_____ you're look - ing for_____ is the

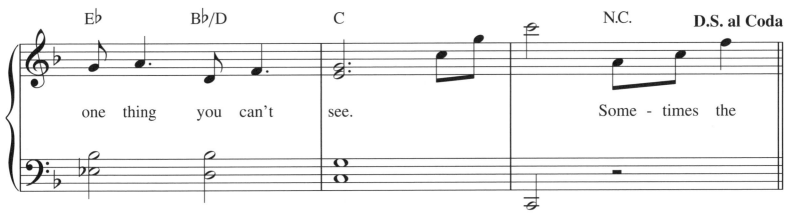

D.S. al Coda

one thing you can't see. Some - times the

CODA

last.

You went and saved the best for last.

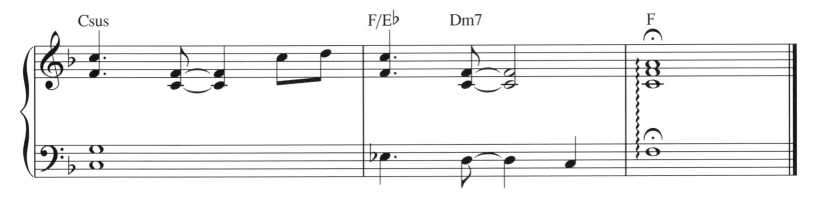

THREE TIMES A LADY

Words and Music by
LIONEL RICHIE

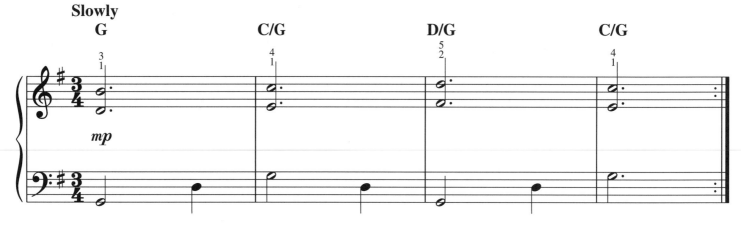

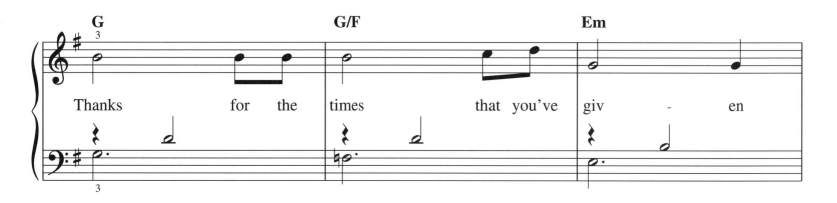

Thanks for the times that you've giv - en

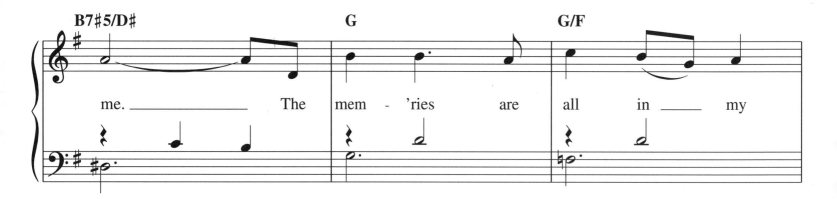

me. _____ The mem - 'ries are all in _____ my

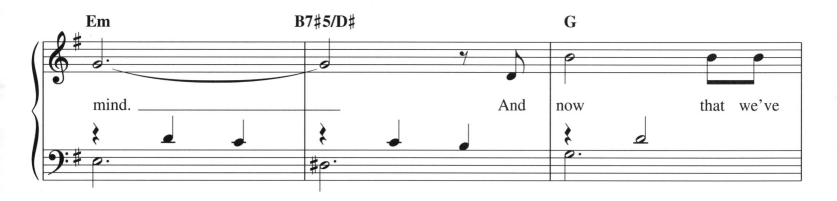

mind. _____ And now that we've

39

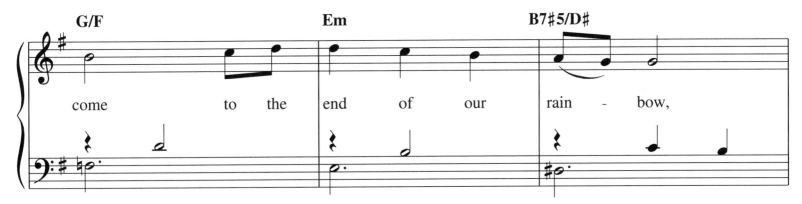

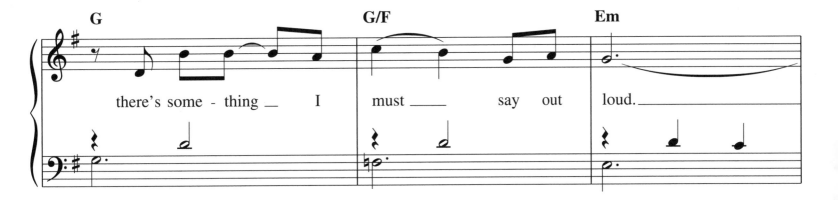

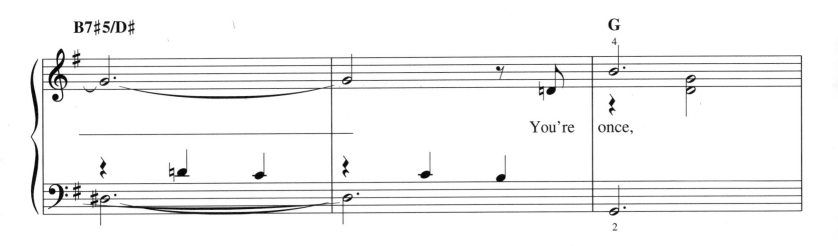

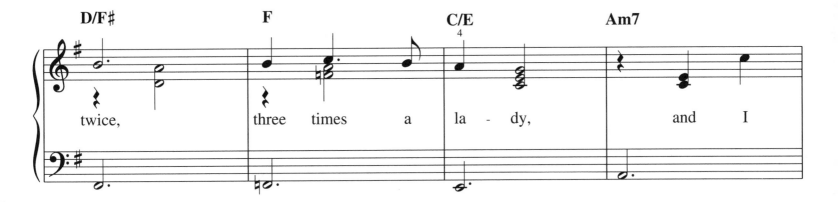

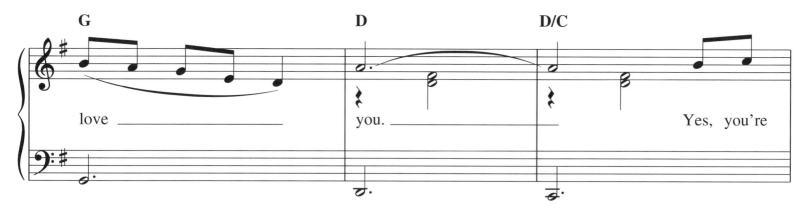

love _____ you. _____ Yes, you're

once, twice, three times a

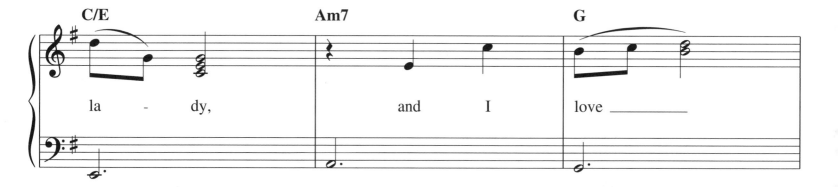

la - dy, and I love _____

you, _____ I

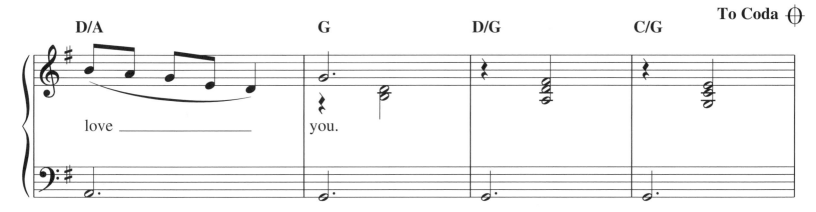

love _____ you.

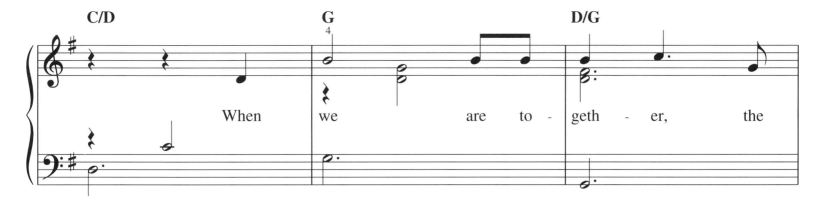

When we are to - geth - er, the

mo - ments I cher - ish with ev - 'ry

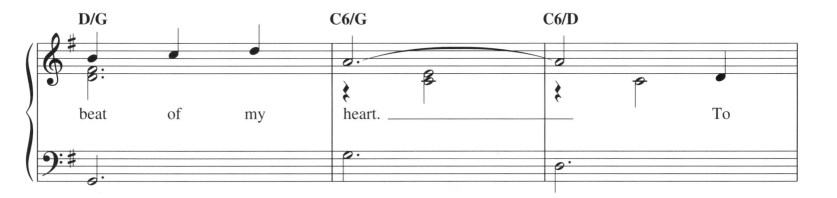

beat of my heart. _____ To

42

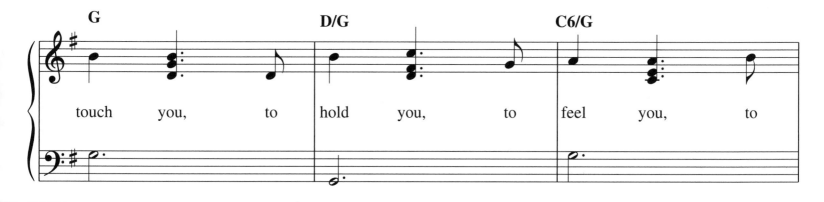

touch you, to hold you, to feel you, to

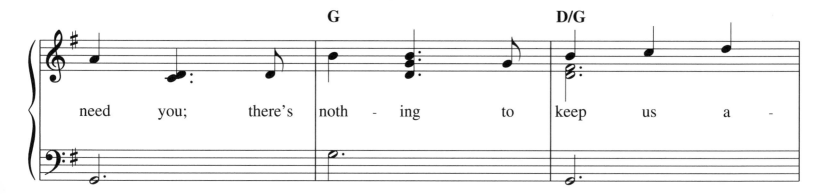

need you; there's noth - ing to keep us a -

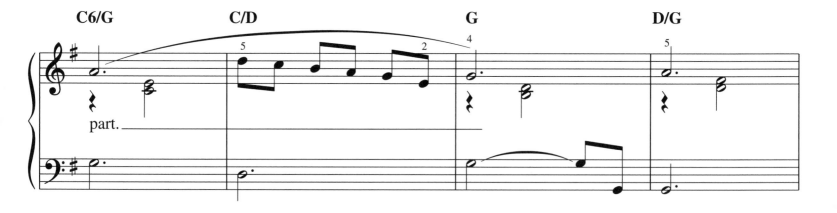

part.

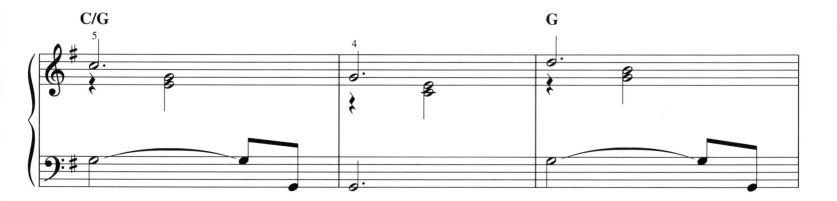

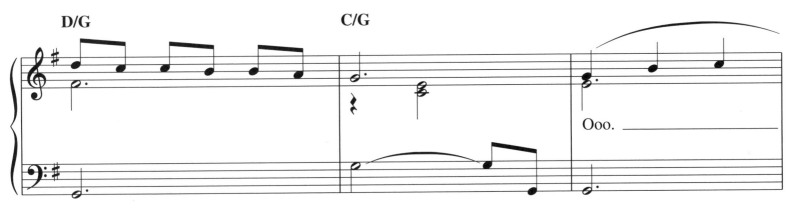

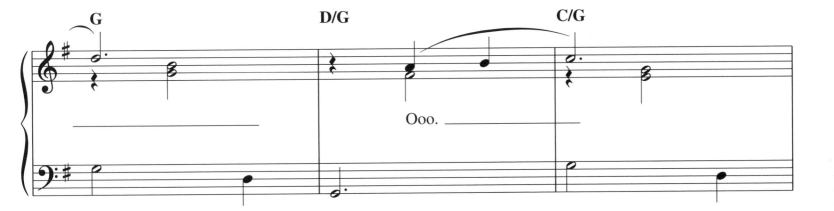

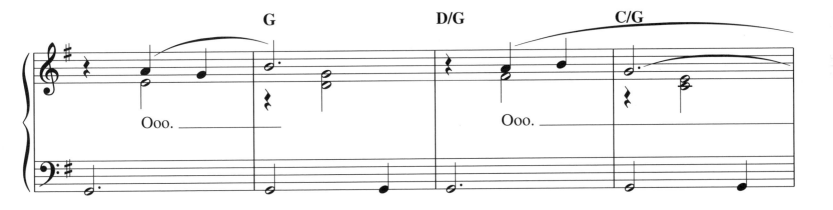

UP WHERE WE BELONG

from the Paramount Picture AN OFFICER AND A GENTLEMAN

Words by WILL JENNINGS
Music by BUFFY SAINTE-MARIE and JACK NITZSCHE

Slow and soulful

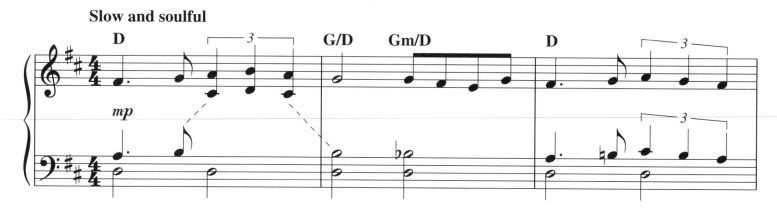

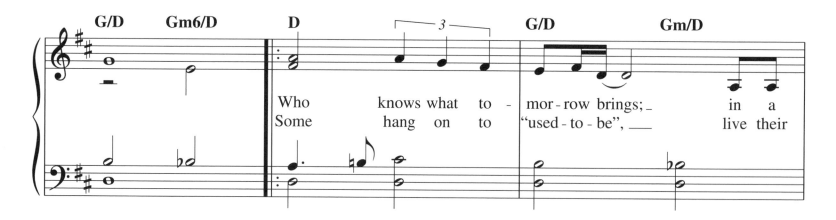

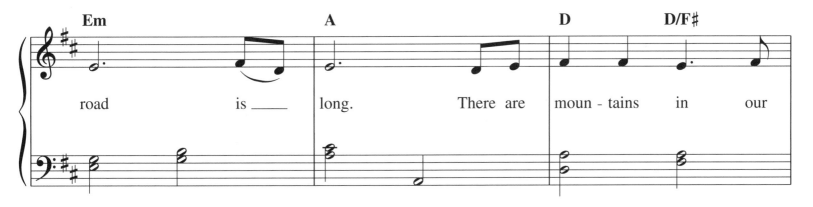

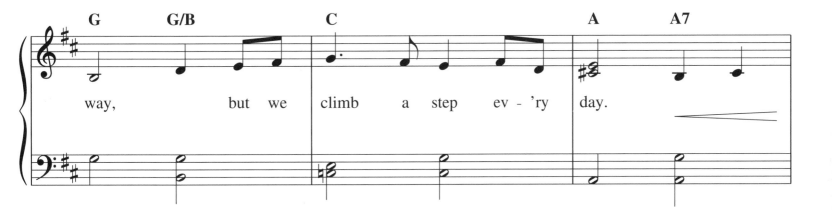

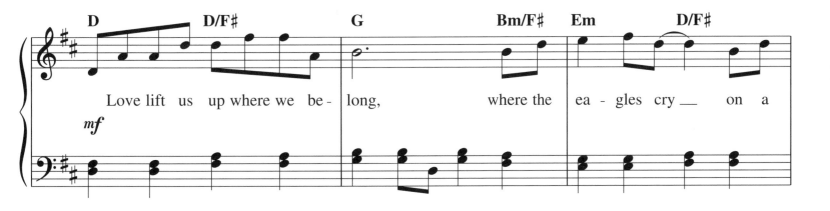

46

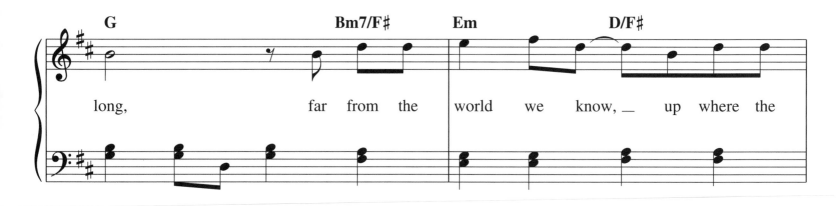

long, far from the world we know, _ up where the

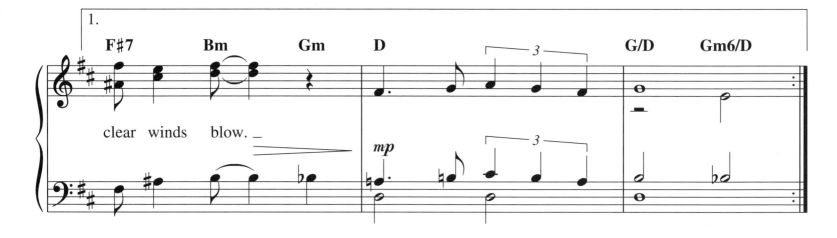

1.

clear winds blow. _

2.

clear winds blow. __ Time goes by, ____

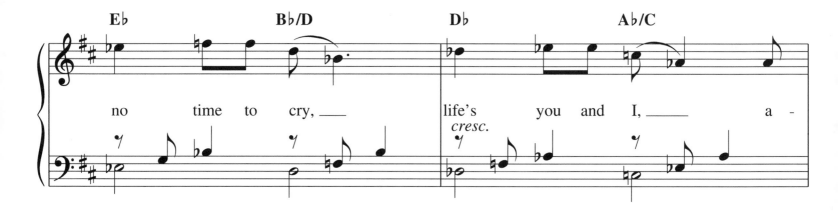

no time to cry, ___ life's you and I, ____ a -

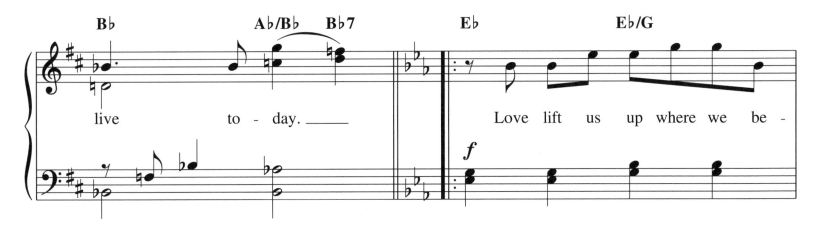

live to - day. _____ Love lift us up where we be -

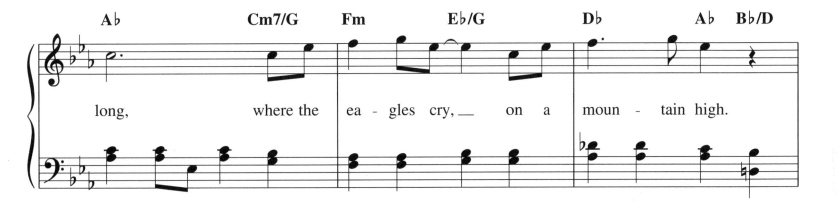

long, where the ea - gles cry,_ on a moun - tain high.

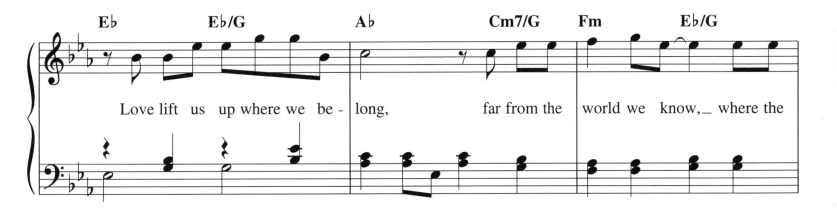

Love lift us up where we be - long, far from the world we know,_ where the

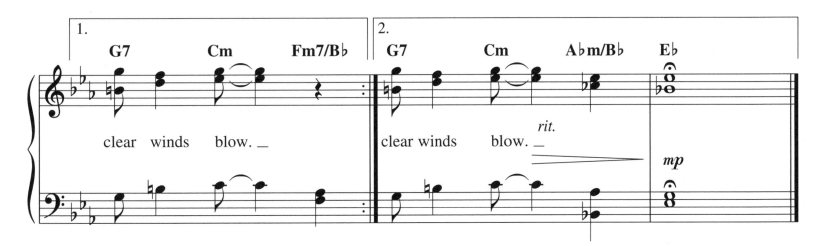

clear winds blow. _ clear winds blow. _

WE'VE ONLY JUST BEGUN

Words and Music by ROGER NICHOLS
and PAUL WILLIAMS

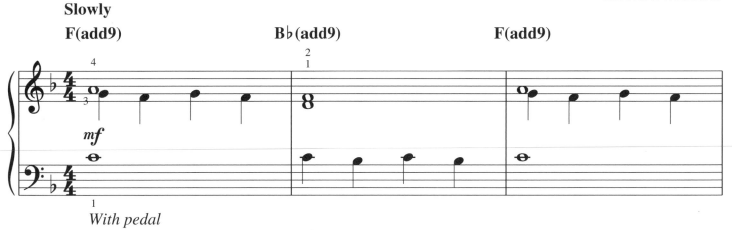

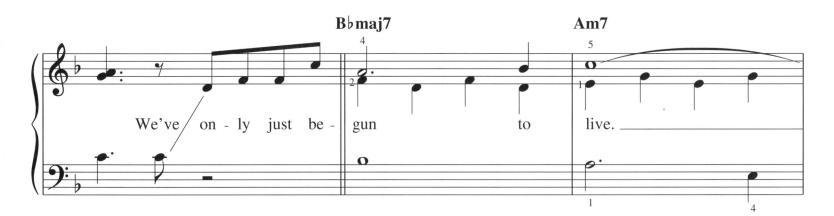

We've on-ly just be-gun to live.

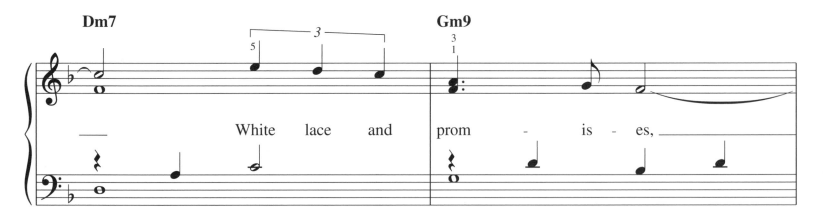

White lace and prom - is - es,

a kiss for luck and we're on our way.

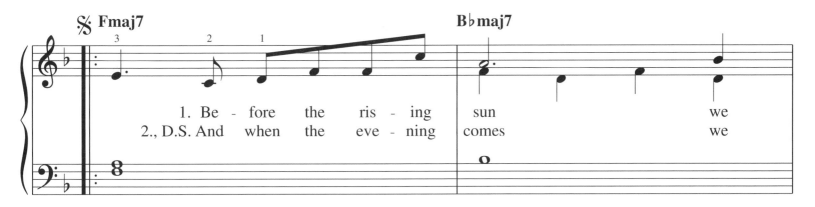

Fmaj7   **B♭maj7**

1. Be - fore the ris - ing sun we
2., D.S. And when the eve - ning comes we

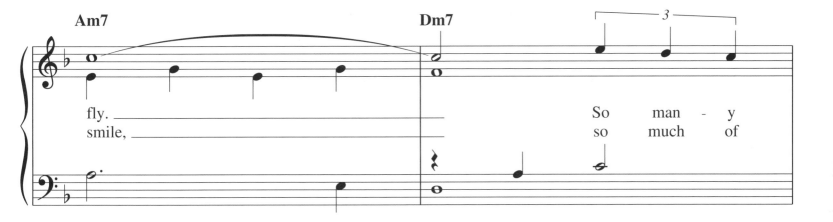

Am7   **Dm7**

fly. So man - y
smile, so much of

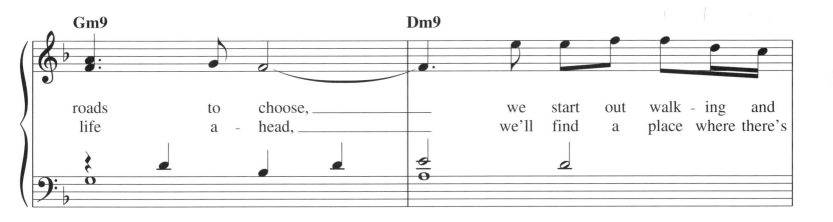

Gm9   **Dm9**

roads to choose, we start out walk - ing and
life a - head, we'll find a place where there's

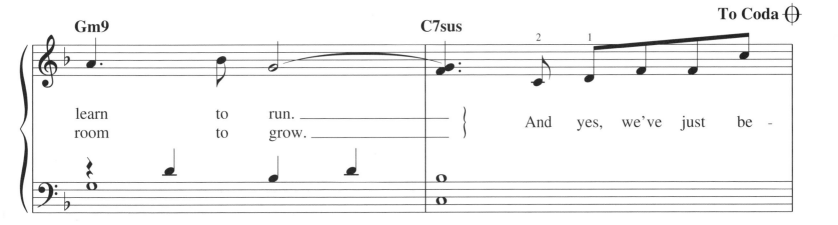

Gm9   **C7sus**   **To Coda** ⊕

learn to run. And yes, we've just be -
room to grow.

50

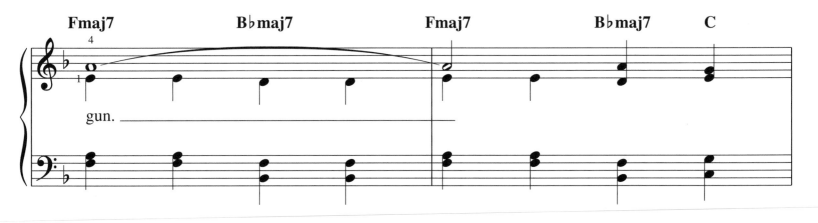

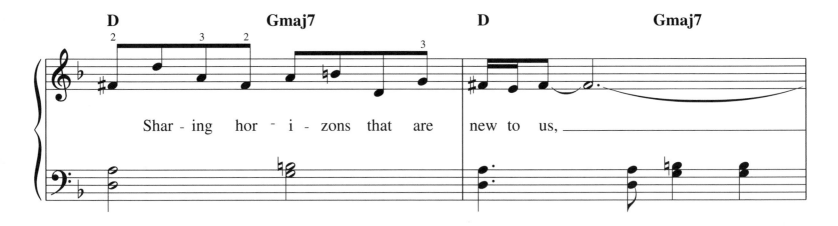

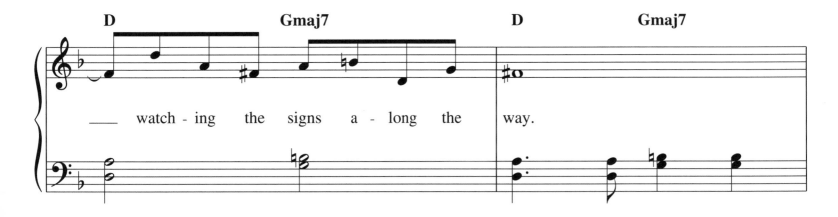

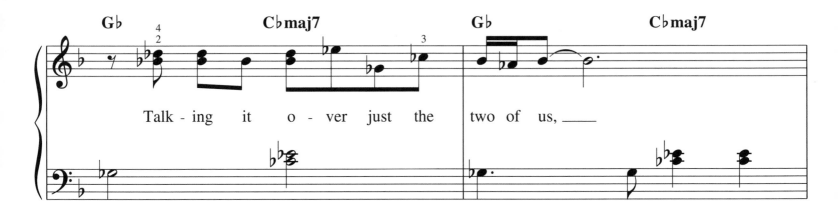

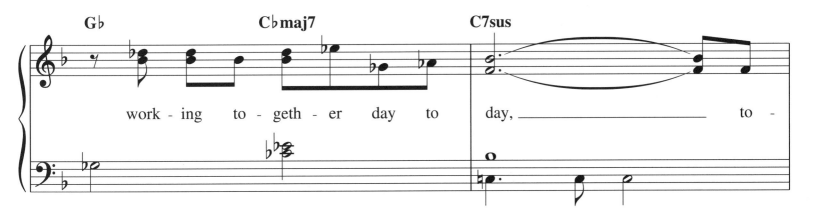

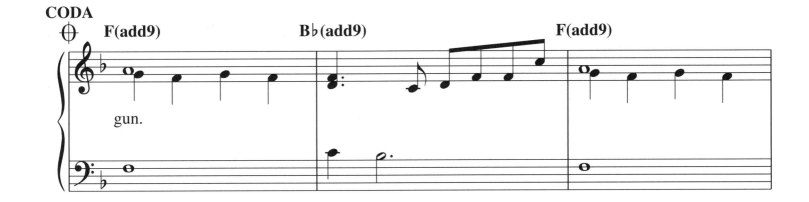

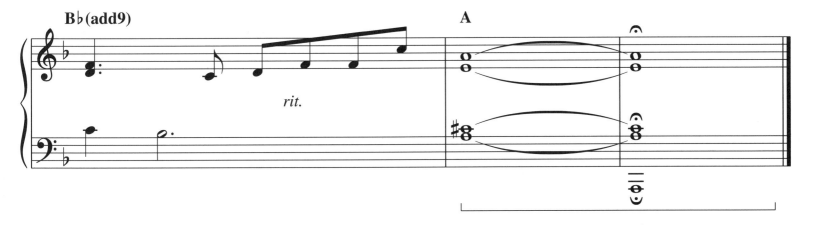

YOU ARE SO BEAUTIFUL

Words and Music by BILLY PRESTON
and BRUCE FISHER

Slow and expressive

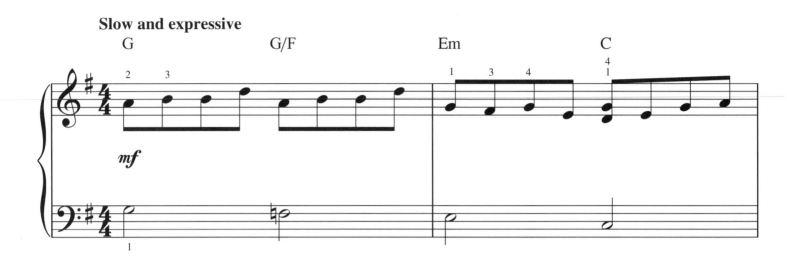

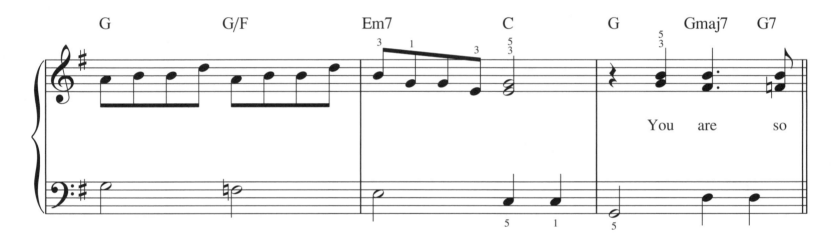

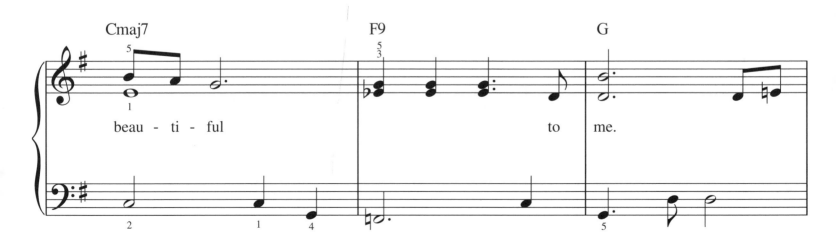

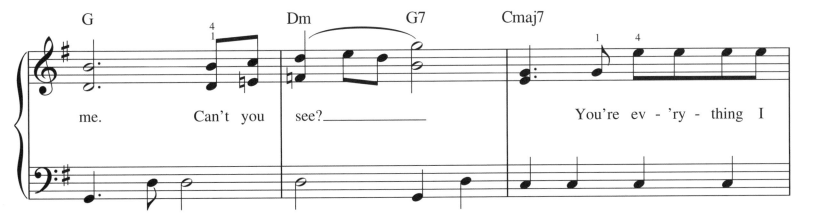

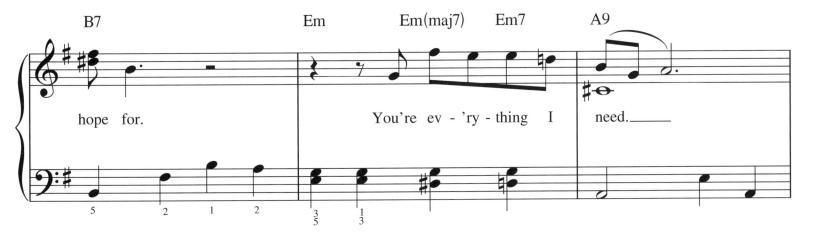

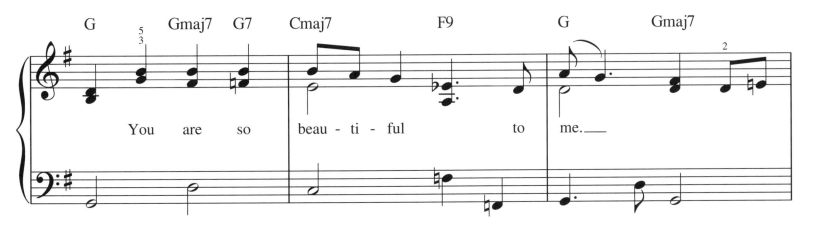

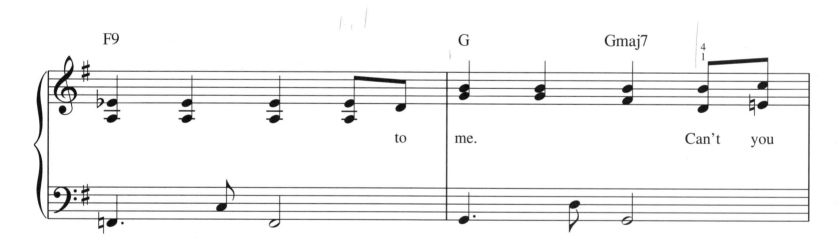

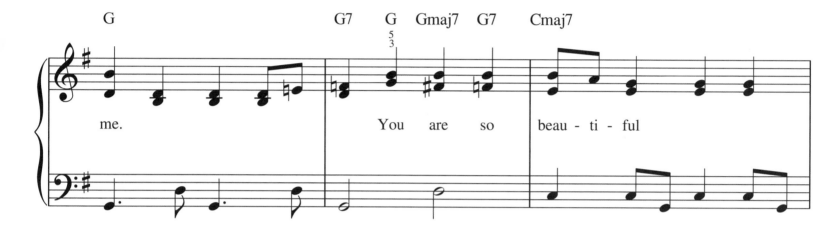

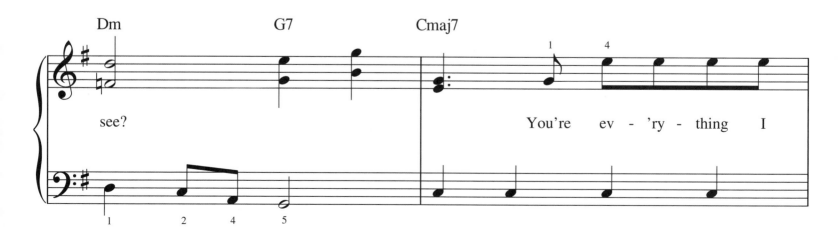

55

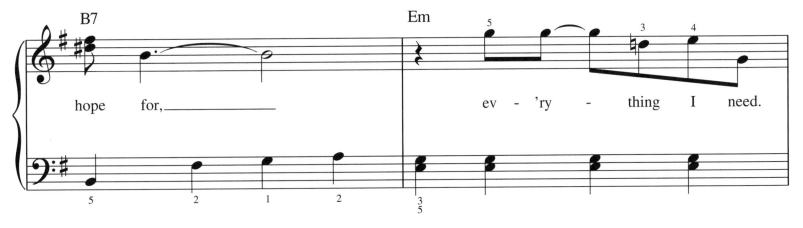

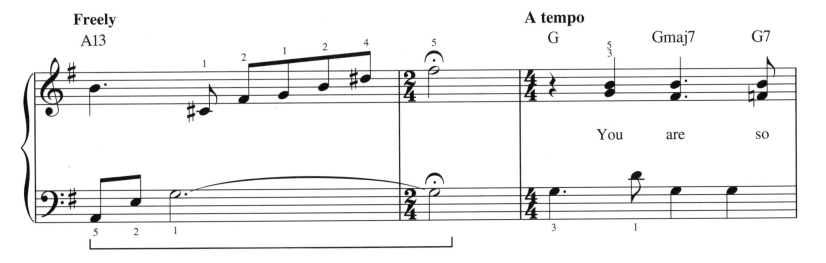

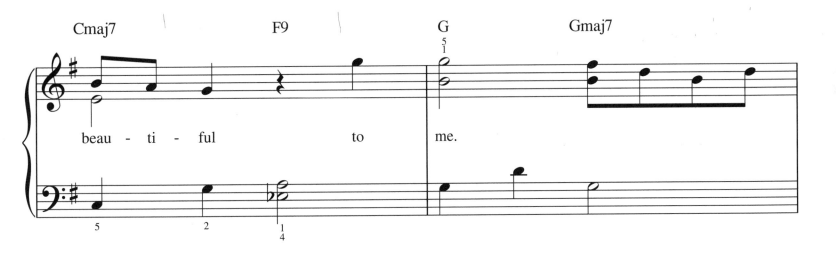

EASY PIANO CD PLAY-ALONGS
Orchestrated Arrangements With You as the Soloist

This series lets you play along with great accompaniments to songs you know and love! Each book comes with a CD of complete professional performances and includes matching custom arrangements in Easy Piano format. With these books you can: Listen to complete professional performances of each of the songs; Play the Easy Piano arrangements along with the performances; Sing along with the recordings; Play the Easy Piano arrangements as solos, without the CD.

GREAT JAZZ STANDARDS
Volume 1
Easy Piano CD Play-Along
10 songs, including: Bewitched • Do Nothin' Till You Hear from Me • Don't Get Around Much Anymore • How Deep Is the Ocean (How High Is the Sky) • I'm Beginning to See the Light • It Might As Well Be Spring • My Funny Valentine • Satin Doll • Stardust • That Old Black Magic.
00310916 Easy Piano $14.95

FAVORITE CLASSICAL THEMES
Volume 2
Easy Piano CD Play-Along
This pack features 13 pieces: Bach: Air on the G String • Beethoven: Symphony No. 5, Excerpt • Bizet: Habanera • Franck: Panis Angelicus • Gounod: Ave Maria • Grieg: Morning • Handel: Hallelujah Chorus • Humperdinck: Evening Prayer • Mozart: Piano Concerto No. 21, Excerpt • Offenbach: Can Can • Pachelbel: Canon • Strauss: Emperor Waltz • Tchaikovsky: Waltz of the Flowers.
00310921 Easy Piano $14.95

BROADWAY FAVORITES
Volume 3
Easy Piano CD Play-Along
10 songs: All I Ask of You • Beauty and the Beast • Bring Him Home • Cabaret • Close Every Door • I've Never Been in Love Before • If I Loved You • Memory • My Favorite Things • Some Enchanted Evening.
00310915 Easy Piano $14.95

ADULT CONTEMPORARY HITS
Volume 4
Easy Piano CD Play-Along
10 songs including: Amazed • Angel • Breathe • I Don't Want to Wait • I Hope You Dance • I Will Remember You • I'll Be • It's Your Love • The Power of Love • You'll Be in My Heart (Pop Version).
00310919 Easy Piano $14.95

HIT POP/ROCK BALLADS
Volume 5
Easy Piano CD Play-Along
10 songs, including: Don't Let the Sun Go down on Me • From a Distance • I Can't Make You Love Me • I'll Be There • Imagine • In My Room • My Heart Will Go On (Love Theme from 'Titanic') • Rainy Days and Mondays • Total Eclipse of the Heart • A Whiter Shade of Pale.
00310917 Easy Piano $14.95

LOVE SONG FAVORITES
Volume 6
Easy Piano CD Play-Along
10 songs, including: Fields of Gold • I Honestly Love You • If • Lady in Red • More Than Words • Save the Best for Last • Three Times a Lady • Up Where We Belong • We've Only Just Begun • You Are So Beautiful.
00310918 Easy Piano $14.95

O HOLY NIGHT
Volume 7
Easy Piano CD Play-Along
15 holiday favorites, including: Deck the Hall • Go, Tell It on the Mountain • God Rest Ye Merry, Gentlemen • It Came upon the Midnight Clear • Jingle Bells • O Come, All Ye Faithful (Adeste Fideles) • O Holy Night • Silent Night • What Child Is This? • and more.
00310920 Easy Piano $14.95

FOR MORE INFORMATION, SEE YOUR LOCAL MUSIC DEALER,
OR WRITE TO:

HAL•LEONARD®
CORPORATION
7777 W. BLUEMOUND RD. P.O. BOX 13819 MILWAUKEE, WI 53213

www.halleonard.com

Prices, contents, and availability subject to change without notice.